# CHECK OUT!

# FORCES AND MOTION

## by Clint Twist

## What makes stuff move?

Copyright © **ticktock Entertainment Ltd 2005**
First published in Great Britain in 2005 by **ticktock Media Ltd.,**
Unit 2, Orchard Business Centre, North Farm Road, Tunbridge Wells, Kent TN2 3XF

ISBN 1 86007 917 2 pbk
Printed in China

# Contents

Words that appear in **bold** are explained in the glossary.

The answers to the questions are on pages 20-21.

# Motion

**Motion** is what happens when something moves from one **position** to another.

This tiger is in motion. He is walking across the snow. Walking is a kind of motion and so is running.

The opposite of motion is **stillness**.

**Now it's your turn...**

The tiger sits down beside the trees.
Now he is still.

Things that are
not moving are
not in motion.
Their positions
do not change.

What do you think will happen to the
tiger's position if he gets up and walks
from the trees to some water?

5

# Pushing

A **force** is something that causes motion.
**Pushing** is a kind of force.

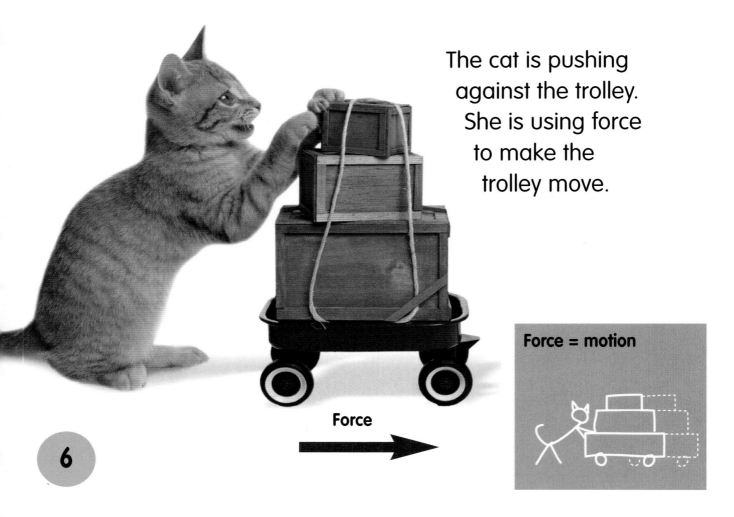

The cat is pushing against the trolley. She is using force to make the trolley move.

Force

Force = motion

## Now it's your turn...

With two cats, there is more force pushing against the trolley.

**More force**

**More force**

Do you think two cats will move the trolley more or less than one cat?

7

# Pulling

**Pulling** is another kind of force.

It is easy to move a **light** or small **load**. The dog can easily pull one small rabbit.

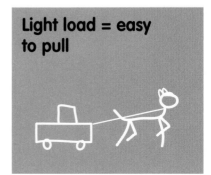

Light load = easy to pull

## Now it's your turn...

**Heavy load**

Do you think the dog will find it easier or more difficult to pull a whole family of rabbits?

# Changes in motion

A moving object does not always move at the same **speed**. It will usually come to a stop.

When the boy rolls the glass marbles, they move quickly at first. Then the marbles start to slow down and they roll to a stop.

Small force = slow speed

## Now it's your turn...

A gentle push, or small amount of force, makes the boy's car move slowly along the table.

**Faster speed**

How do you think the boy can make his car move faster?

# Slopes

**Slopes** have an effect on the way things move along them.

This bear is **sliding** down a slope covered in snow. The steeper the slope, the faster the bear slides.

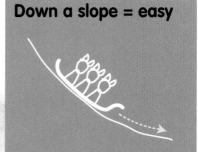

Down a slope = easy

## Now it's your turn...

These dogs are pulling a sledge that slides over the ground.

**Up a slope**

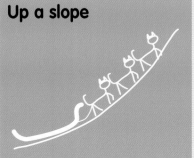

Do you think pulling the sledge up a slope will be easier, or more difficult, than going down a slope?

13

# Friction

**Friction** is a force that stops things from moving easily. There is friction when one thing slides against another.

Snow has a **smooth** surface with little friction, so things slide easily.

Snow slope =

*easy to slide*

Grass has a **rough** surface and there is a lot more friction than with a smooth surface like snow.

Do you think it is easier, or more difficult, to slide down a grass slope instead of a snow slope?

**Grass slope**

# Changing shape

Force doesn't just make things move. Force can also change the shape of some objects.

When working with **dough**, you use force to push and pull the dough into shapes with your hands.

Small force = small shape change

# Check it out

## Now it's your turn...

When you push your finger gently against a piece of modelling clay, you make a small dent.

**Bigger force**

If you push with more force, does the dent get bigger or smaller?

# Changing direction

We can use force to stop a moving object,
or to change its **direction**.

When the goalkeeper
catches the ball,
he is applying a
force with his
hands. The force
stops the ball
from moving.

Force = can stop motion

A tennis player uses force to change the direction of a moving object.

The boy throws (pushes) the ball up into the air. Then he applies a force with his tennis racquet to hit the moving ball.

What happens to the direction of the ball when the boy hits it?

# Answers

## Page 5

If the tiger walks from the trees to the water, his position will change.

**Motion = changed position**

## Page 7

Two cats will move the trolley more than just one cat by itself.

**More force = more motion**

## Page 9

The dog will find it more difficult to pull a whole family of rabbits because a heavy load needs more force to move it.

**Heavy load = difficult to pull**

## Page 11

The boy can make his car move faster by using more force – giving the car a harder push.

**A hard push (more force) = faster speed**

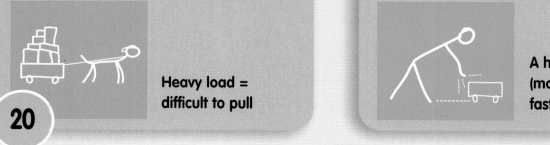

## Page 13

Pulling the sledge up a slope will be more difficult because it needs more force to move an object up a slope than down a slope.

**Up a slope = more difficult**

## Page 15

It is more difficult to slide down a grass slope because there is more friction to stop easy movement.

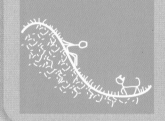

**Grass slope = difficult to slide**

## Page 17

If you push with more force, the dent will get bigger. Using more force causes more change in shape, or movement.

**Bigger force = bigger shape change**

## Page 19

By applying a force with his racquet, the boy hits the ball over the net. The direction of the moving ball changes.

**Force + moving object = can change direction**

# Glossary

**direction** A line that points towards the final position of a moving object.

**dough** A mixture of flour and water that can be baked into bread or pizza.

**force** Something that causes movement, such as a pull or push.

**friction** A force that slows down movement.

**light** Something that does not weigh very much. The opposite of heavy.

**load** Something that is moved from one place to another.

**motion** Another word for movement.

**position** The place where an object is in relation to other objects.

**pulling** A force that is applied from in front of the object to be moved.

**pushing** A force that is applied from behind the object to be moved.

**rough** A surface with many bumps.

**sliding** A movement that takes place when two surfaces are touching.

**slopes** Lines or surfaces with one end either higher or lower than the other.

**smooth** A surface that has no bumps.

**speed** The rate at which an object moves over a distance.

**stillness** When nothing is moving.

23

# Index

## Picture credits

t=top, b=bottom, c=centre, l=left, r=right, OFC=outside front cover
Corbis: 4, 12, 13, 18, 19. Powerstock: OFC, 1, 2, 3, 5, 6, 7, 8, 9, 10, 11, 14, 15, 16, 17, 22, 24.

Every effort has been made to trace the copyright holders, and we apologise in advance for any unintentional omissions. We would be pleased to insert the appropriate acknowledgements in any subsequent edition of this publication.